The Undying Faith Book 4. A Guide to a Life of Success and Happiness

The Undying Faith, Volume 4

Hebert McQuinn

Published by Hebert McQuinn, 2022.

While every precaution has been taken in the preparation of this book, the publisher assumes no responsibility for errors or omissions, or for damages resulting from the use of the information contained herein.

THE UNDYING FAITH BOOK 4. A GUIDE TO A LIFE OF SUCCESS AND HAPPINESS

First edition. July 19, 2022.

Copyright © 2022 Hebert McQuinn.

ISBN: 979-8201748593

Written by Hebert McQuinn.

Table of Contents

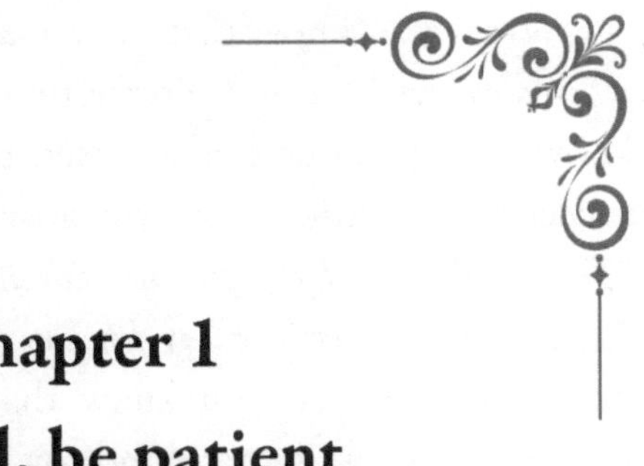

Chapter 1
Be still, be patient

The Psalmist says in Psalms 46:10-11: "***Be still, and know that I am God; I will be exalted among the heathen, I will be exalted in the earth. The Lord of hosts is with us; the God of Jacob is our refuge.*** " We are commanded to be still, in the knowledge that He is God. Being still comprises in being calm and tranquil, being silent. It also means being motionless, hushed. Now all of the foregoing definitions as related to a person's state of mind portray a picture of peacefulness ensuing from self-assurance and inborn confidence.

Knowing that He is God, we are not emotionally stressed about the lateness of the hour or about what people are beginning to say about us and our situation. We are not stressed about anything at all, in our knowledge that He is God.

What does this knowledge entail? You might ask. The knowledge that He is God means the acknowledgement of His stature, acknowledgement of the fact that He is the one who was before the beginning of time, who still is and forever will be. It entails knowledge of His Omniscient, Omnipresent, and Omnipotent nature. It entails the knowledge that with Him, nothing is impossible.

When you know that your matter is in the hands of one who is everywhere at the same time, who has all power and all knowledge, you don't have reason to fear or doubt its eventual successful resolution. Then you are able to say with the Psalmist: "*The Lord is my light and my salvation; whom shall I fear? The Lord is the strength of my life, of whom shall I be afraid?* No one indeed. When you know that you have power of such humongous magnitude behind you, lighting your way and giving you strength and courage, you simply have no reason to fear anything. You can be still, and know that He is God.

Now there are times, and there will be times in your life when you have prayed for something and that thing is not manifested in the physical world yet, and you see no sign at all that the manifestation might happen anytime soon. You may have hinted to some people in your life your intention with regard to the acquisition and possession of the thing that you desire to acquire and possess or with regard to becoming this particular person you want to become. Or you might have acted in a way that indicated to people around you your intention to acquire that thing which you desire or to become what you desire to become.

The longer it takes for you to acquire the object of your desire, the more attention you will receive from people around you, especially your enemies. The pressure that you will be feeling will be mounting with every passing day. And naturally you will be getting more anxious and worried as time progresses with your dream not materializing.

It is important to acknowledge the fact that whatever we do in the world we do not do in isolation, with no context at all. We do the things we do in the midst of other people, some of whom would be loving and supportive whilst there would be others who would be hateful, antagonistic and critical of us and our projects.

The longer it takes for the desire to be realized, the more pressure you will feel, that is if you are a person who doesn't have a lot of faith. The delay in the realization of a dream tests the patience and resolve of the dreamer. Sometimes it just takes holding on, hanging in there and not losing faith in the possibility of your eventual success.

I remember reading somewhere that God's delays are not denials. You don't necessarily have to see any signs that guarantee the eventual fulfilment of your desire for you to keep believing in its ultimate fulfilment, when it's all said and done.

You have to stubbornly hold on to the belief that things will work out and that you shall live to see the day when your desire is finally realized. Don't stop believing that your Heavenly Father will never let you down, and that when you ask Him for bread, He will never give you a stone and when you ask Him for fish, He will never give you a snake.

The challenge with fulfilment of a desire is the time that elapses between when you pray for its fulfilment and the time that such fulfilment actually happens, the intervening period of time between the saying of the prayer and the answering of the prayer. It is in this intervening period that the dreamer's patience is tested at times, because some things are just not going to happen at the time when we expect them to happen.

We have ample scriptural illustrations of this fact. The Bible tells us that one Joseph, the son of Jacob, dreamt two dreams on two separate occasions when he was still just a small boy. The interpretation of his dreams by his father was that there was coming a time when Joseph will be so great that he, his wife and Joseph's brothers will bow down before him. The dreams meant that Joseph would in time be that great. For obvious reasons those dreams of his did not endear him to his brothers, they became jealous and hateful when they heard about them.

He was still only just a small boy when he dreamed those dreams and they only came true when he was a grown man already. There was this long intervening period between the dreaming of the dreams and their realization, and in the meantime life was happening to him.

One of the events that occurred in between the dreaming of the dreams and their realization was his brothers threw him in a deep dark pit and left him there to die a solitary death. They threw him in that pit, a very lowly place it was indeed, where they left him to eventually meet his death.

Now, the dreams of a person who is thrown into a pit which he has no way of coming out of, are obviously as good as dead, that is, in accordance with normal human expectations, the dreams will die with the dreamer when the time comes for him to eventually die.

That pit he was thrown into was supposed to ultimately become his grave, if his brothers were to have things their way. There was no way out for him and for a long while he sat brooding in that pit that was to be his dying place in accordance with his brothers' plan. It was deep and it was dark. He was positioned lower than where everyone else was in in the world. Everyone was on higher ground above him.

His erstwhile dreams were about his parents had his brothers bowing down before him one day in his lifetime when he would have become great. But here he was in a deep, dark pit, left there to die a lonely death. There was no way his parents and brothers would somehow come and lower themselves into this pit so they could bow to him, so to him this must have been reassuring as it would have meant that if his dreams were still certain to come true, then that the pit would certainly not become his grave. The scenario in the dreams did not take place in a deep dark pit. If the dreams were indeed still to come true, it meant only one thing for sure, that somehow he was going to get out of the pit.

And as fate would have it, the same people that threw him in the pit were the ones to eventually get him out of it. One of his brothers, Juda, who wasn't completely sold on the idea that he should be left to die a lonely death in the pit, bargained for his rescue from the pit with a plan he conceived when he saw some people coming their way.

He managed to convince his brothers to get the younger brother out of the pit and sell him as a slave to the passers-by. His brothers saw the financial sense in his plan and were convinced that that was the way to go. So they got him out of the pit and sold him for a few shillings.

Now on his way to the land of Egypt with his master, Joseph's dreams seemed so far away and completely out of sight. The fact was that at that time his status was that of slave. He was the lowest of all men, with only one thing in his favour, he was out of the pit now and on higher ground with everyone else. His current condition though was in stark contrast to one in which he could reasonably expect anyone to bow to him. Who in their right mind would bow to a slave?

But then, unbeknownst to him at the time, that was not to be what's finally settled for him. When his master got to Egypt he sold him to Potiphar, one of the king's officers, who was the captain of the palace guard. He was sold as a slave to a new master, and clearly his dreams were still verily and truly out of sight. He was in a space wherein it would have been easy for him to give up on his dreams and resign himself to the fate of just being a slave. It would have been easy for him to just accept slavery as a condition he was destined for anyway, and the dreams to have been just a form of night entertainment of long ago..

His life conditions and circumstances were surely not those of a person that people could travel long distance to bow to. But God had not forsaken nor forgotten Joseph. He was with him and made him successful in everything he did in his master's house.

Potiphar noticed that the Lord was with Joseph and made him successful in everything, and so he was pleased with him and made him a personal servant in charge of his house and everything he owned. Joseph's conditions and personal circumstances then changed for the better, but he was still only a personal servant to an Egyptian king's officer.

And then the unthinkable happened while he was in this position in Potiphar's house. His master's wife falsely accused him of attempted rape and Potiphar had him thrown in jail as a result. He was now no longer a slave but a prisoner, jailed for an alleged attempted rape of his former master's wife. He was then just a lowlife, and time was not standing still.

He seemed as far away from realizing his dreams as he could possibly be. Surely now the reasonable thing to do then was for him to fold the tent of his dreams and move on. The reality was that he was a prisoner in a land far away from home and no one ever bowed to prisoners, on the contrary, prisoners bowed to the prison authorities as a rule. He was the one bowing to others.

A long period of time had elapsed from the moments spent in the pit and Joseph was nowhere near the realization of his dreams. But God had not deserted him. The jailer was pleased to realize that Joseph was blessed by God and he put him in charge of all the other prisoners and made him responsible for everything that was done in prison. The Lord made Joseph successful in everything he did in that prison but his status hadn't changed. He was still just a prisoner, though he now had more rights and privileges.

And then perchance, two of the king's officials were thrown in jail and they found Joseph there. And then one night they each dreamed a dream, which they told Joseph about in the morning. Joseph interpreted their dreams and things happened to them as Joseph had said they would, in his interpretation.

They were eventually released from prison, the king ordered that one of the be executed and the other reinstated to his job of being a wine steward, just as Joseph had said when he interpreted their dreams. Joseph had asked the wine steward to be kind enough to mention him to the king when things were going well for him. Clearly Joseph saw an opportunity for himself in his relationship with the wine steward and took the initiative to ask that favour of him. There was a glimmer of hope for him at last.

And mention faim to the king the wine steward did eventually, after two years had passed. So many years had passed between his being thrown in the pit and two years after the release of the wine steward from prison. A less determined person would have just resigned himself to prison life and left it at that. But Joseph was entertaining hopes of an early release from prison already. From when the wine steward was released, Joseph was living in hope and God did not disappoint him. He was being still and reassured God still loved him.

One night the king of Egypt dreamed two dreams that none of the people he trusted could interpret. That was when the wine steward mentioned Joseph to the king as a dream interpreter of note. The king immediately called for Joseph to be brought before him. Long story short, Joseph was able to interpret the king's dream and thereby won himself an early release from prison.

Not only that but the king appointed him prime minister of all of Egypt and made him second in charge to him. He entrusted Joseph with the governance of the country because he realized that God was with him. The success of Egypt as a state lied in Joseph's hands.

Surely Joseph must have been aware at this point that his dreams were beginning to take shape and were very close to being realized. And then finally it did come to pass in the course of events that his father, mother and brothers came to Egypt and bowed to him, Joseph the prime minister of Egypt. The man in charge, second in command only to the king.

By telling this story I'm trying to bring home to the reader one biblical illustration of the value of patience. The intervening period between Joseph's dreams and their realization was to be measured in years. And his life conditions and circumstances in the intervening period were not commensurate with those of a person on track to realize his dreams. The lesson in the story is that no matter how long it takes for your dream to come true, no matter how insurmountable the obstacles in your way may seem to be, you should hold on to your dreams and never give up on them because God does not work according to the ways of human beings. He has His own way of doing things and no matter how rough the ride may turn out to be, we should keep our faith and at the right time He will deliver us from the dreadful conditions to the ones we dreamed of. We should learn to be still and know that He is God, no matter what the crisis may be that we would be facing at any given point in time.

He knew that He was going to make Joseph the second most powerful man in Egypt but he got him to that position in a round about manner. Perhaps just to show us that He can lift you up from the darkest doldrums to the highest heights you can dream of, if you only believe and not give up on your dreams when your conditions change for the worst. That it doesn't matter how dire your situation may seem, if you single-mindedly believe in your dreams and are willing to go through the storms of life to get to the point of their realization, they will come true. If you would just be still and know that He is God.

The other Bible story that clearly illustrates this same principle is the one of David. He was fifteen years old when he was anointed by the prophet Samuel but he was only to become king when he was thirty years old already. And in the intervening fifteen years a lot happened in his life that made the realization of his dream, which was God's promise to him, seem highly unlikely. In the intervening period he had his running battles with Saul, who was the incumbent king of Israel at the time, because he, Saul wanted to kill him.

Between David and the realization of his dream stood a murderous king who wanted him dead. In their clashes the king had the advantage of being a king and all the power and resources that goes with the title. So it was not a fair duel at all where the two of them were concerned. David had to go through experiences where his death was almost a certainty, only to escape and survive by the skin of his teeth each time. He had to persevere and exercise patience to get to the point where he would ascended the throne and be crowned king of Israel.

It is not everything that you plan on doing that is going to happen as you want it to or at the time that you expect it to. In the intervening period you will be having to deal with all kinds of trials and tribulations and forces that would seek to distract you, take you off your course, and derail your dreams.

It's okay in the process to be cool about everything. To be still and know that He is God. Anxiety, despair and constant worry are for people who do not have enough faith. In Luke 1:37 we read the following: *"For with God nothing shall be impossible."* One who puts his/her trust in Him has the confidence to ride the storms of life and withstand the delays that may come without being deeply shaken.

We would further do well to remember what is written in Mark 9:23: *"Jesus said unto him, if thou canst believe, all things are possible to him that believeth.* "This is a powerful statement of truth from the great teacher. In the intervening period between your dream and its realization, don't ever stop believing. The challenges, obstacles and problems you'll encounter along the way will only be opportunities for you to prove yourself and the might of God, nothing more.

And then there is the story of that man, Moses. The man who is credited with being arguably the greatest leader the Israelites have ever had in biblical history. The story of Moses epitomizes patience as an essential character trait of a great leader. The Bible tells us that God told Moses in no uncertain terms that although He was sending him to the king of Egypt to negotiate for the release of the Israelites from the bondage of slavery, so that they could then leave Egypt and journey to the land which God had promised them, and that He was going to make the king stubborn and not inclined to fully cooperate with Moses and negotiate in good faith.

So all the while Moses was negotiating with the Egyptian king he knew that he was not going to let the Israelites go until he had no choice left but to let them go. Moses was shuttling between God and the Egyptian king for a long time, honestly trying to get the king to release the slaves, while knowing very well that the king was going to be stubborn and that God, who was sending him to the king to plead with him, was the one making the king stubborn.

Moses had to be patient with both God and the king and dutifully carry out God's instructions. In the end his patience paid off because matters did eventually get to the point where the king gave in and agreed to let the Israelites go. Through the challenges he was still and knew that God was God.

Life does at times put us in situations where we have to exercise patience whether we like it or not. When you enrol for a B-degree at a university, for instance, you have to be prepared to study three years or longer in order to obtain your degree.

In order to obtain the degree and graduate, you have to deal with the study material and do many hours of reading and studying. Three or more years must elapse before your dream can come true and there is no way that it can happen in a shorter period of time. Those who are patient and work diligently eventually make it to the graduation podium.

Some things you just can't succeed in without having to exercise patience. Cricketers playing a test match know that they may have to wait up to five days to know who the winner will be and by what margin they will win the test match. The same goes for the fans and supporters of the game. They have to follow the proceedings religiously for a number of days to find out who the winner will be in the end and what the final score will be. Now that is a sport for patient people if there ever was one. Though it takes a long time for a test match to be concluded, for those who have the patience, cricket is a most enjoyable sport.

The same goes for the sport of golf. It's also not a game that is concluded in a day but for its enthusiasts it's the most enjoyable sport, they don't mind that they have to follow the game for days to know who the winner will be. There are certainly some benefits to being a patient person.

Patience is something that we have to learn and cultivate within ourselves because it is an indispensable virtue in ensuring success in many of our endeavours. Many of our dreams in life take time to materialize and require of us to be patient. When a couple are expecting a baby there is no way yet to speed up the process by which a baby comes into the world. There is only the long nine month waiting period which at times comes with a whole lot of challenges.

So in this situation we have to exercise the utmost patience and in the end we will be rewarded with our bundle of joy, if it's meant to be. If you are a person whose patience is not well developed, those nine months can feel like nine years. People who are not patient, who want everything to hurry up and get done, are a generally stressed and anxious lot who are uptight and desperate for the better part of their lives because life generally does not happen according to anyone's timing.

That brings to mind two conversations I heard listening to a radio show recently where the host asked people to call in and talk about encouragement by other people that didn't work for them. The first was a man who said that he hadn't had employment since he left high school six years previously and that people kept telling him to be patient and not give up because things will work out for him in the future. They were telling him to hang in there, so to speak.

He said that he considers those words of encouragement water off a duck's back as that is what people have been saying to him the past six years, so he didn't expect anything to change this year because of those same words of encouragement.

That made me so sad because his attitude was so negative at a time when he needed to approach his situation with a more positive mental attitude. He ran out of patience so he just gave up on his dream, which would perhaps be okay if he had a plan B that he had decided to pursue. He had waited six years and so felt justified in giving up at this stage.

I asked myself, he's given up, so what is he going to do going forward? For all we know he could be giving up at a time when God was about to answer his prayers, who knows? The Israelites journey to Canaan could be travelled in four days, the experts tell us, but it took them forty years because God doesn't do things like humans do, He has His ways that are not like the ways of humans. At all times, in all situations we would do well to remember that and keep it in mind.

For all we know, he could have given up on job hunting to try his hand at crime just when things were about to change for him, when what he has been looking for for six years was just around the corner. He might find himself in prison, not knowing how close he was to achieving his goal when he made the about turn to a life of crime. How long is long enough we will never know if we turn our backs on our dreams before they are realised.

I sincerely hope that he didn't go this route though I don't know what else people do when they give up on their dreams, do they commit suicide, maybe? I don't know, but either way a person is better off waiting patiently for his chance to come, if he has no viable alternative that is. The man should have just been still and know that He is God.

The second caller was a woman who thought her chances of finding a man of her dreams and getting married have all but vanished into thin air because of the age she was at the time. She talked in resignation about her biological clock and was generally just negative about her situation. Listening to her I was very disappointed. Being an unmarried forty year old woman is not a very uncommon thing in life and it most certainly doesn't mean that the curtain has gone down on the prospect of marriage for good. People fall in love all the time, there is no age limit.

I remember some time ago I was watching television and they were broadcasting a wedding of an elderly couple who had met in an old age home. They were around seventy years old and looked very happy and content as they went about the festivities. I know people who have experienced childbirth at fifty years of age. I was struggling to understand what the lady's problem was exactly. And thinking about it I couldn't rule out the reality that her problem could be attributed to a negative self-image and very little faith.

The other thing I know is that it's not really about the wording of the encouragement but more about your attitude towards the encouragement itself, that determines whether it has a positive impact on you or not. I remember once in my life I was feeling so overwhelmed and crushed by life's problems that I was merely just surviving and wondering if I would ever get the breaks I needed in life. I was in the doldrums.

I was walking down some street in my hometown one day when I met a former work colleague of mine I had not seen in a while. We exchanged greetings and engaged in some small talk and suddenly he stopped, looked in my eyes, smiled and said "Buddy, things don't always happen at the time we expect them to, and even then they happen, they don't all happen in a day, we have to learn to hang in there for the duration of the processes and give positive things space to happen naturally. "

To this day I don't know what Josiah saw in me that day that prompted him to give me that little motivational speech. All I know is it had a reassuring effect on me. He spoke as if he could see through my façade right into the depths of my soul. Then we said goodbye and went our different ways.

I don't know if my friend knows it but those few words he said to me were life changing for me. I was so encouraged by those words because they made me feel that I was not alone in the world in what I was going through and I felt strengthened and revitalized. I had a new energy about me and I faced life with renewed vigour after that talk. And I found that with my change of attitude life became a little bit easier. There was a spring in my step and a new determination about my personality.

I been recharged and to this day my friend's words would come to mind each time I felt like things were not moving along fast enough and they would invariably make me feel stronger and more resilient. So when people tell you to be patient it is no more about what they are saying than it is about your attitude to it when you hear it.

In Hebrews 6:15 we read the following about Abraham: *"And so, after he had patiently endured, he obtained the promise."* God had made a promise to Abraham, and then some time passed before God delivered on His promise. In the intervening period we are told that Abraham had patiently endured.

From the time that you conceive your plan and set about implementing it to the time when it finally comes to fruition, there is the intervening period which you must navigate. There are difficulties associated with the plan that you must endure until the time comes for the plan to come to fruition.

This is the period in which weaker willed people, unable to exercise patience and perseverance, change their minds and start something new, sometimes just when they are about to have their breakthrough. The thing about this attitude is you will never know how close you are to realizing your dream if you don't exercise patience and endure till the end..

In Hebrews 10:36 we read: *"For ye have need of patience, that, after ye have done the will of God, ye might receive the promise. "* We are in this verse encouraged to do our part with patience while we wait for God to do His in the fulfilment of His promise to us. He did say that He would not leave nor forsake us.

He is on our side and with Him nothing is impossible. We have this guarantee to help us muster the patience required for us to reach the point where God's promise to us is fulfilled. There is no bypassing the requirement for patience, whatever it may be that you want to see manifested in your world. Most things take time to manifest.

In Romans 8:25 we read the following: *"But if we hope for that we see not, then do we with patience wait for it."* That which we see not is what has not appeared in the objective world yet, it is that which we can still only see with our mind's eye. Although we may be seeing it clearly in our imagination, though the mental picture of it be vivid, it is not manifest in the objective world where we can interact with it with our physical senses yet.

We have to be patient and wait for the time when it will be objectified in the physical world. Because He art great that is in us and with Him, nothing is impossible. No matter what the one who is in the world may say or do, we wait patiently, nothing and no one can make us panic or doubt. We, with patience, bide our time and know that He is God.

In Psalms 40:1 David says: *"I waited patiently for the Lord; and He inclined unto me and heard my cry."* There are benefits to waiting patiently even when we may even be crying. We cry in the hope that He will hear us. If we hang in there and exercise patience, in the end He will answer. He will deliver to us the object of our desire. We would do well to keep in mind always that His timing is not like ours and that His delays are not denials. Yeah. We have to learn to wait patiently for him to deliver us, and to believe that He will hear our cries.

In Psalms 37:34 he says: *"Wait on the Lord, and keep His way, and He shall exalt thee to inherit the land: when the wicked are cut off, thou shall see it."* Those who wait on the Lord are those who put their trust in Him in everything they do. They pray to Him for help in having their desires fulfilled. The land is a symbol of prestige and opulence. Those that wait on Him He rewards with an inheritance of opulence and luxury untold, if that is what they ask of Him. That is if they wait and keep His ways, some of which we will discuss later in the book. In the meantime, rest assured, you can never wait in vain, waiting on Him.

Isaiah says in Isaiah 40:31: "*But they that wait upon the Lord shall renew their strength; they shall mount up with wings as eagles; they shall run, and not be weary; and they shall walk, and not faint.* " I am not going to quote any more verses to corroborate the evidence provided in the ones I have already quoted, of the immense benefits of waiting on the Lord. During the waiting period, life happens to the person waiting, invariably things will happen to him/her that test his/her faith, and in the time it takes for his/her desire to be realized, his/her patience, being an important part of his/her faith, will also be tested.

He gives strength and resilience to those who put their trust in Him. No matter how hard the knocks of life may be on one that waits upon Him, he/she will always bounce back and carry on with what he/she needs to do for his/her dream to come true. He/she is never discouraged, no matter what catastrophe might befall him/her in his/her quest to realize his/her dream. God gives him/her the ability to endure and persist until he/she emerges victorious in whatever endeavour he/she may be engaged in at any given point in time. He truly is a God of winners. Be still, and know that He is God.

Chapter 2
Learn to persevere

The topic of perseverance is closely related to the one of patience, in that while patiently waiting for the realisation of their desire, people are usually put through trials and tribulations that seek to shake and undermine their faith, which bring with them unfavourable conditions, circumstances and hardships under which they must persevere in order to succeed. These trials and tribulations are the occurrences that separate the goats from the sheep. The Bible implores us to always endure with patience until the promise is realized and the salvation of the Lord is upon us.

Now, salvation is the act of saving a person or thing from something, someone, conditions or circumstances. We often times find ourselves in situations that cause us grief and pain, both physical and emotional. And at the same time we have the ideal situations that we desire for ourselves, that we would rather be living in. When we wait patiently and persevere, our salvation will come, when the Lord would save us from our current situation which is tormenting us and deliver us into the one we have been tearfully longing and praying for.

Because of the close relationship between the concepts of patience and perseverance, the biblical examples wherein their individual value is illustrated are mostly the same. The story of Joseph for instance, is one of those that illustrates the value and benefits of perseverance. The Bible tells us that Joseph was put through all kinds of trials, tribulations and adversities but he persevered throughout, until his dreams were realized.

He persevered from the situation in the pit into which he was thrown and left to die a lonely death, through the situation of being a slave, through the one of being a prisoner and right up to the point where he ascended to the second highest office in Egypt. We are taught in the story to hold on to our dreams and keep believing in them even when they seem impossible to realize anymore, to persevere until God's plan for us comes to fruition.

In the story of David we learn that same lesson. David could have run away from Saul and lived in exile in relative peace and safety. He could have easily given up on ever becoming king because of Saul's hatred and frequent attempts to kill him.

He has had also had to lead the Israeli army in many battles where his life was at risk. He was not preoccupied with the fear of death because he trusted God to deliver on His promise to make him king of Israel. The adversities he has had to face were nonetheless very real and they were testing his faith in God. He patiently persevered, biding his time until he ascended the throne to be crowned king of Israel.

In Luke 1:24 we read the following: "*And after those days his wife Elisabeth conceived, and hid herself for five months saying {1:25} Thus hath the Lord in the days wherein He looked on me, to take away my reproach among men.* "We are told that this is what ensued after Elisabeth discovered that she had conceived and was pregnant at the age where she was not expected, even by her husband, to bear any children. She was an old childless woman who in her own words was the scorn of her community. Before she conceived she has had to deal with her reproach among men, in her own words.

I can imagine that at the time of this occurrence, there were women who were very proficient at conceiving and giving birth, women who were well renowned for their special ability in this area of life. But as we know by now, God's ways are not like our ways and His thoughts are not like our thoughts. So when He chose a woman to give birth to the great John the Baptist, He chose the barren Elisabeth, perhaps to reward her for her perseverance, after she had endured the scorn of her community and tribe for a long time.

She persevered and in the end was given the unique honour of giving birth to an extraordinary human being. There are great rewards for those who persevere. You will never know how your unsavoury situation was meant to end if you give up prematurely. Just never give up.

You could be going through your own barrenness in some area in your life where people have given up on you and are not expecting you to succeed anymore. You may also be subject to scorn and contempt from fellow human beings because of that spell in your life.

They may be laughing at you and your hitherto futile attempts at making the grade in your chosen field of endeavour. You may have been reduced to a laughing stock in your community. Your situation could be analogical with Elisabeth's literally or figuratively. It doesn't matter. If you keep your trust in

God and hold on, He will save you from that unsavoury situation and deliver you into ideal one you that desire.

Our God is not a God of people who give up. He is a God for whom nothing is impossible. If we call ourselves Christians and say that we believe in Him, we are not honest and truthful with ourselves if we have instances where we give up on our dreams because they may be taking longer to come to fruition than we had expected them to.

When we allow ourselves to doubt His ability to save us from situations that are less than ideal for us and to deliver us into the ones that we desire, we are not being righteous people that know how to walk in faith. Surely if you have in your corner a Being of unlimited power and ability, you shouldn't fear anything or doubt your abilities. But it is easy to give up and fail if you allow yourself to doubt His power for whatever reason.

Jesus himself is a prime example of how to persevere under the pressure of constant criticism, hateful jibes, touting, scorn and plotting by people that don't love you and don't want you to achieve your life's purpose. He persevered under difficult conditions created by the enemies of his faith and continued to do the work that his Father sent him to do regardless. He suffered their ignorance, was patient with them and persevered until he had accomplished his mission.

We should also be that single minded and focused about things we consider to be of importance to us. We shouldn't allow ourselves to be distracted and diverted from pursuing our goals by negative criticism and societal pressures. We should brace ourselves to take these pressures in our stride and remain focused on and faithful to our dreams until they are realized. Perseverance is the mother of success, I've heard it said. I can't agree more. Without it we cannot have success on a grand scale consistently.

Jesus further exemplified the value of perseverance when he was being tempted by the devil. When he had not eaten for forty days the devil advised him to ask God to turn stones into bread so he could eat, but he refused to take the easy way out and take the advice of the devil to have his hunger satisfied. He was very hungry but he persevered. He endured the hunger and trusted in God until he defeated the devil.

The devil is very good at offering us these easy ways out of situations that test our patience and resolve, and constantly whispers in our ear that the often unsavoury situations that arise out of our efforts to execute our plans are not worth our perseverance, and that attempting to endure them is not worth our while.

Giving up is easy. Sometimes when we embark on a particular project we may be unrealistic about the degree of difficulty with which it can be executed and finished. We sometimes only realize when we are in the middle of the project that it is more challenging than we had envisaged prior to commencing work on it. The tougher the challenges become, the stronger the temptation to give up, turn our backs on the project and call it a day.

It's easier to stop trying and accept defeat than to hang in there and give your best even in the face of unrelenting pressure from people opposing your efforts and people just criticizing and trying to break your spirit. You have to learn to persevere if you are to succeed in making your dreams come true.

In whatever venture we may wish to undertake, we have to take cognizance of the fact that not everyone will be supportive and encouraging, that we are sure to meet with and have to deal with fierce opposition along the way. People will try to discourage you when they see that you want to achieve something that is going to make you a better person, there will always be that kind of people who will try to trip you, who will try to stand in direct opposition to you on your path to success.

I know there are people I was working with at previous my previous place of employment who became worried when they heard that I was studying law part time at the University of South Africa. I was working full time as a Traffic Officer at the time. I remember there was a time when I dreaded going to work because of the fierce criticism and hateful insinuations I faced daily, with people passing derogatory remarks when they see me, laughing me to scorn and making all kinds of silly remarks.

It was a very hostile, stressful and frustrating environment that I had to experience every working day. I knew that I had to face the situation head on and not flinch if I was to win the fight I found myself in at the time.

It wasn't easy having to deal with the difficulty of my studies and my negative colleagues at the same time and at some stage I had, at the time, to be hospitalized with a stress related illness that almost ended my career. Upon discharge from hospital I was more determined than ever to complete my degree.

I continued from where I had left off when I was hospitalized. I resisted the temptation to give up on my dream in the face of all the pressures I was subjected to. I told myself that the pressures were appropriate training as I would be subjected to worse in my work as a lawyer.

I told myself that though it was unpleasant, I had to get used to working under that kind of pressure. I went on to complete my degree regardless of all the negativity that surrounded me at the time. I laughed last and I laughed best because I persevered.

Chapter 3

Learn the art of persistence

After perseverance, persistence is the logically the next topic for me to tackle. In Luke 11:15 we read the following: *"I say unto you, Though he will not rise and give him, because he is his friend, yet because of his importunity he will rise and give him as many as he needed."* Jesus was teaching people about the value of persisting when one has a desire he/wants to be fulfilled, when one has a need that he/she wants satisfied.

He made a parable about a person who has friend visit him at night, having no bread to give his visitor he goes and knocks on his friendly neighbour's door to ask him for bread. The neighbour is initially irritated and refuses to get out of bed to help his friend out.

But the man at the door kept knocking and persisting in asking for bread for his night visitor and eventually, because of his importunity the neighbour got out of bed gave him the bread that he needed. Importunity consists in making persistent requests. A person acting with importunity is unyielding and uncompromising in his/her approach. He/she is never going to let up until he/she is given what he/she wants. If the person to whom the demand is directed is unwilling to meet it, he/she will have to put up with the unrelenting attitude with which it is being made.

That speaks to being single minded about what we want and not taking no for an answer. Our mental attitude should be one that says we are not leaving until we get what we want. Our focus and attention is on the object of our desire exclusively. Everything else is relegated to the background and what is uppermost in our mind is getting what we want. The attitude of Importunity speaks to persistence in seeking what is important to us. If we are resolute and persistent in seeking it we will invariably find it, whatever it may be.

This concept speaks to not being half-hearted in our effort to realize our dreams. We must pursue our goals with the stubbornness of a pitbull dog. Only people who are this resolute in their approach succeed in achieving worthy goals. These are people who are not easily dissuaded once they have made up their minds to go after a certain goal. Jesus teaches us that with this kind of attitude we will never go wrong. He teaches us to be single minded and unyielding when in pursuit of our goals. I once read somewhere that much water wears the marble.

You are most likely to be given what you want if you insist without yielding. Moses was importunate in his demand to the king of Egypt for the freeing of the Israelites from slavery so that they could leave Egypt. The king's refusals and changes of mind were many but Moses did not relent. He was always back the next day making the same demand. It had to get to a point where the king finally gave in and let the Israelites go.

From Jesus's parable we learn that we must not be easily dissuaded from demanding what we believe we should be given.

That sometimes you may be given what you want for no reason other than your importunity in demanding it. I believe that even in prayer we should not be relenting in our belief in the ultimate fulfilment of our desire in the form of an answered prayer.

Our conduct must be one of importunity, not in the sense of being a source of irritation to God with constantly repeated prayers, but in behaving every day from when we finished our prayer as though we have received what we were praying for already. We are taught to behave resolutely in fostering a mental attitude of thankfulness and joy for our imagined receipt and possession of the object of our desire.

In Luke 18:1 we read the following: "*And he spake a parable unto them to this end that men ought always to pray, and not faint; {18:2} Saying, There was in a city a judge, which feared not God, neither regarded man: {18:3} And there was a widow in that city; and she came unto him, saying, avenge me of mine adversary {18:4} And he would not for a while: but afterward he said within himself, Though I fear not God, nor regard man; {18:5} Yet because this widow troubling me, I will avenge her, lest by her continual coming she weary me. "* Here Jesus is making another parable to the people. Again seeking to illustrate the power of Importunity.

The unjust judge in the parable did in the end grant the importune widow her wish and avenged her even though he initially wouldn't take heed of her cries. The point Jesus was making was that if a man that was clearly unjust and stubborn eventually gave in to the incessant requests of the widow, we should not have doubt in God's willingness to and inclination to hear our cries when we cry to him for help. It is said that we should pray without ceasing and by continuous prayer and supplication bring our petitions to Him.

All that is meant with the parable above is we must live a prayerful life if we are to have a beneficial relationship with God. I guess one could say that we must be so prayerful that our individual voices become a familiar sound in His ears as opposed to just saying a once off prayer and forgetting about Him.

Prayer must of necessity be incorporated into our lifestyles so that a prayerful life gets to define who and what we are. Jesus himself was an example of this kind of life. He never ceased to call upon his Father and made it plain that he and his Father were one, inseparable. Communication is very important in any relationship and in our walk with God we communicate with Him in prayer, prayer is the medium of our communication with Him.

Because communication is essential to any relationship, thoughts and feelings must be expressed on a continuous basis for the relationship to be workable and beneficial for those involved. Therefore if we say that we are Christians, we have to be seen to be following the example Christ set for us and live our lives according to his teachings. We have to try and form a closer relationship with our Heavenly Father for our supplications to be considered favourably each time.

The reader will have realized that the chapter on perseverance and the one on persistence are shorter than the one on patience. This is so because they are both closely related to the topic of patience, and I did write extensively on most of what is involved in both concepts in the chapter on patience so I didn't want to repeat those same things in discussing each of those two topics, what I sought to do is to write on the topics only about those things that I have left out in my discussion of patience. This was necessitated by the interrelatedness of the three topicss in the context in which I discussed them.

Chapter 4
Meeting the spiritual requirements

In 2Corinthian 4:3 Paul says the following: "*But if our gospel be hid, it is hid to them that are lost {4:4} In whom the god of this world hath blinded the minds of them which believe not, lest the light of the glorious gospel of Christ, who is the image of God, should shine unto them.* " Paul tells the Corinthians that the gospel of Christ is in plain sight for everyone who believes to see and find but is at the same time impossible for those who do not believe see and to find. The light of the glorious gospel of Christ is the truth that sets people to whom it is revealed free

Who are those who do not believe? You may ask. They are those who are spoken of in the scripture as the carnal man, the natural man who walks by sight. By whom it is said that the things of the Spirit of God cannot be discerned. To whom, it is said that such things are foolishness. In these two verses the apostle Paul tells us why this is so. He says that the god of this world has blinded their **minds,** not their eyes, mind you, but their minds, so that they wouldn't see the glorious gospel of Christ should it perchance shine on them.

The gospel of Christ shines on everyone indiscriminately, but only those who believe see and find it because by believing they have outsmarted the god of this world and are beyond his reach. For him they are the ones that got away. When I wrote about belief in one book in the series, I specifically mentioned that it is as fundamental as it is foundational to be Christian faith in particular and to religion in general. It is through belief in God's existence and in His rewarding of those who diligently seek Him that He can be found by those who come to Him.

It is hardly surprising then that Satan uses this character trait of belief to identify those whose minds he should blind. This is how the thief steals from them their potential to discern things of the Spirit of God and renders them oblivious and unresponsive to the light of the glorious gospel of Christ, should it by any chance shine on them.

Belief is the weapon by which to break the stranglehold of the devil and avail yourself to your heavenly inheritance as a child of God. In the part that follows, I want to attempt to shine the light of this glorious gospel on everyone that believes, please, allow me

In Ecclesiastes 10:19 we read the following: "*A feast is made for laughter, and wine maketh merry: but money answereth all things.* "I thought we should start here, that this should be our point of departure. A lot of things have been said on the subject of money and a lot will continue to be said but in Ecclesiastes 10:19 above, that is what is said about money. That everything else is for certain specific purposes, but money is made for answering all things. Not some things but **all things.**

No one can live in avoidance of money, it is simply impossible to do so. We need money and we cannot live without it. We need money to pay for all things that that we want and all things that we need. Everything in the world can be reduced to a sum of money, even the land and everything underneath it can be obtained for a sum of money. This is a very important and powerful item for a person to possess and the more of it he/she possess the better life will be for him/her. That is a fact in most cases.

There is a monetary price on everything in life. To live a high quality life one needs to have a lot of money no doubt. But then just how much is a lot of money is a question that can only be answered subjectively. The appetite for this all-important commodity varies from person to person depending mostly on the individual's attitude towards it.

It is a fact that there are some people who have voluntarily taken and some who continue to take a vow of poverty, supposedly for religious reasons. These people fall mostly in the category of those who believe strongly that money is the root of evil and for this reason are not very affectionate towards it.

I must contend, on a personal note that this is a very unfortunate view of money. I'm not judging anyone, God knows I believe firmly that everyone is entitled to their own opinions. I'm only saying that money is a very important item to have in this world. Some would argue that it cannot buy love and hey, there are just so many things people say about money.

But I know that there are people from whom love gets withdrawn when they run out of money so I'm not sure about the validity of the argument about money not being able to buy love. Homes have been broken when the money ran out, and spouses divorced each other for financial reasons. So that is the negative effect that lack of money can have on people who are in love, the very same love that it supposedly can't buy.

Lest I diverge from my topic, let me point out that it is the insane love of money that is the root of all evil and not money itself. Jesus himself did need money to live and did honour his financial obligations by payment with money. At one time when he was asked to pay his taxes he sent a disciple to go fishing and to look for the money in the mouth of the first fish that he would catch. He used that money to pay his taxes.

When you love money so much you are willing to trade your soul for it then you have an unhealthy relationship with it. Yeah, it all boils down to the kind of relationship that a person has with money. That determines to what lengths he/she would go to access it and how much it can corrupt him/her.

And it is possible to have the kind of relationship with money wherein you are in charge of and in full control of your emotions where money is concerned, this kind of relationship with money I believe to be healthy. It is also possible to have the kind of relationship with money wherein money is in charge and fully in control of your emotions, which relationship I believe to be unhealthy.

I don't want to go into the things that the insane love of money makes people do daily, the world over. That is not the reason I introduced the topic. I introduced it because I want to talk about wealth, of which money is an overarching symbol. I want to talk about some of the requirements that need to be met for one to be favoured with material wealth by God, bearing in mind that the definition of wealth is also a subjective question.

Just to emphasize the importance of money I want to take the reader to Matthew 25:34-36 wherein Jesus says : "*Then shall the King say unto them on his right hand, Come, ye blessed of my Father, inherit the kingdom prepared for you from the foundation of the world:{25:35} For I have hungered, and ye gave me meat: I was thirsty, and ye gave me to drink: I was a stranger, and ye took me in:{25:36} Naked, and ye clothed me: I was sick, and ye visited me: I was in prison and ye came unto me. "*

Only people who are generous and have the money to be able to express that generosity can do all of the above. Although you may be of generous predisposition, if you do not have the money to do anything for anyone you are no better than those who have it but do not give, your generosity is empty and meaningless.

Those who inherit the kingdom prepared from the foundation of the world do not include those who only wish that they could feed the hungry, give drinks to the thirsty, take strangers in, clothe the naked and do any or all of the things Jesus mentioned as qualifying people for the great inheritance.

So if we want to be worthy of the inheritance of the kingdom, we must be in a position to be able to give generously to the poor and needy. Giving to them according to their needs must be something that is affordable to us. We therefore must acquire the resources necessary, for us to be able to accumulate enough money for our own needs as well as that extra that we can spare in helping those who are in need of our help.

In the end we are not going to be judged on how much money we have or how much wealth we have been able to accumulate but on how we have deployed our resources, especially in regard to the poor and needy. The glorious gospel of Christ expects no less of us than to be our brother's keeper.

In order for us to be thus positioned we need to remember that we are the children of the Most High, the Creator and owner of all there is, and that by default we are the heirs to His infinite kingdom. If our problem is that we do not have money or that the money that we do have is not enough for us to be able to make a difference in the world, Jesus says all that we have to do is ask, and it shall be given unto us. Whatever we want we have to we ask for in prayer and it shall be given unto us.

The same power that enabled Jesus to feed thousands with two fish and a five loaves of bread will in similar abundance answer our prayers for what we need to be able to live with abundant generosity. And the Lord our God is always willing and able to give us what we want because when we gain more ability to do good in the world we do so for His glory.

Now there are those of us who follow the doctrine of tithing and those of us who don't. Those who tithe have their reasons for doing so in as much as those who don't have their reasons too. The topic of tithing is one of those topics that invariably stir up controversy when it's up for discussion. And I can understand why it gets people highly emotional in the world of today.

The Bible tells us that God, through His prophets, communicated rules and regulations for the practice of tithing. He issued instructions on how exactly tithing should be effected. And these instructions were issued in the context of His church in the Jewish community wherein there was a hierarchical structure of church priesthood and leadership.

The church had the Levites, the priests and the sons of Aaron who were tasked with various duties and responsibilities in the church. And it is to these individuals that the tithes were distributed, according to God's instructions. In addition there were the musicians and porters that also had to have their share of the tithes. And there were a whole lot of ceremonies and rituals that went with the process of tithing.

With that said, in most of the Christian churches of today, there is no hierarchical structure similar to the one the Jewish church had when God made the rules about tithing to it. Tithing was, as I understand it, a religious practice that was peculiar to the Jews as a nation. One may argue that that ceased to be the case with the coming of Jesus Christ and his gospel, through which the gentiles became joint heirs with the Jews in the kingdom of God. That is all good and okay.

The problem which some raise regarding tithing as practiced in most churches today is that what is done there is merely adaptations and different versions of the original concept of tithing. It is a fact that some of the churches today have no hierarchical leadership structure to speak of so all the tithes are for the consumption of one person who is the head of and sometimes even owner of the church. There is no one else sharing in the consumption of the tithes.

Also, the other bone of contention for those who are against the concept of tithing as practiced currently is that it is not practiced as part of a package of religious rituals that were practiced at the time God decreed it. That the Christian church of today no longer makes animal sacrifices, nor does it engage in celebrations and feasts that must characterize the festivities surrounding the practice of tithing.

I do not know what your take on the above topic is or what your personal stance is regarding this all important religious practice of tithing. All I know is that with faith, everything is possible. I also know that nothing is impossible for him who believes. I also believe that as we think in our hearts, so we are. So for me it is not so much about the practice itself as it is about the thought and belief behind the practice.

Be that as it may, in Malachi 3:10 we God says to His people: "*Bring ye all the tithes into the storehouse, that there may be meat in mine house, and prove me therewith, saith the Lord of hosts, if I will not open the windows of heaven, and pour you out a blessing, that there shall be no room enough to receive it..*" That my friend, was God's promise to those who tithe.

He was challenging us to test Him and tithe as He had decreed and see if He would not bless us above and beyond our expectations. He says that there will not be enough space to accommodate the blessing He will open heaven's windows to pour out to us.

He can do the same for you as an individual, since in most churches today tithing is individualized. Just pay your tithes in the way that you believe in your heart to be correct, ignore the intellectual arguments surrounding the practice and you will be blessed in accordance with your belief.

And then when you will have been blessed like that you will certainly be able to bless others with your possessions who may approach you in need. And there is a rule from God about how this giving to the poor and needy should be done.

It is to be found in Matthew 6:1-4. The verses read as follows: "*Take heed that ye do not your alms before men, to be seen of them: otherwise ye have no reward of your Father which is in heaven. {6:2} Therefore when thou doest thine alms, do not sound a trumpet before thee, as hypocrites do in the synagogues and in the streets, that they may have glory of men. Verily I say unto you, They have their reward. {6:3} But when thou doest alms, let not the left hand know what thy right hand doeth: {6:4} That thine alms may be in secret: and thy Father which seeth in secret himself shall reward thee openly."*

We are advised to give our charity donations in secret where men's eyes don't pry. According to this advice we should not give to the poor and needy for the sake of being seen and praised by people. There is a contemporary trend by those who have donations to make to the poor to summon the media to come, witness and report on their charitable donations to the poor and needy so that their pictures should grace the pages of social media. When they give something to someone they want the whole world to know about it. There is something that is off about this attitude and I'll tell you what it is.

I remember a time in my country, back in the year 2020 when we went into a hard economic lockdown to fight the spread of the Corona virus. The government put in place very stringent restrictions on commercial activities and movement of people at that time.

We were in essence all put under house arrest. We were only allowed to leave our homes only and strictly for the purpose of purchasing essential household items and medicines. Businesses that sold what was not considered essential for our survival were all ordered to close shop for twenty one days initially.

Among those affected were poor people who sold all kinds of merchandise on the street sidewalks. They were also ordered to close shop. There was this local politician who took this as an opportunity to show everyone how caring and generous a person he was. He invited the local newspaper to take photos of him handing money to some of the street vendors that were affected by the lock down measures. Some of the pictures taken at that event were posted all over social media.

It is precisely this type of giving to the poor and needy that we are all warned in the verses above against doing. Whether or not the whole thing was a political ploy is beside the point because part of what was intended by it was a solicitation of praise for the publicly generous man.

Everyone was made to see what a good person he was, how kind and generous he was to the poor. Now we have to take note of the fact that we are not told that this is wrong, only that the people who give this way have already had their reward and can expect nothing from God. The recognition and high praise by the people watching the spectacle is their due reward.

The other instant that comes to mind is something that happened at a funeral of a former work colleague of mine who at some stage in his life was destitute for whatever reason. From the time I first knew him he was wheelchair bound. The speakers in the funeral program took turns to pay tribute to the man and related how well they knew him and shared some fond memories with the rest of us.

And then there was this particular speaker who spoke glowingly about his relationship with the deceased and when he was done, he mentioned a time when he apparently visited the deceased's house and found that there was no food in the house, he told us how he apparently went to buy him chicken portions at a local store.

Granted he did a good deed for a friend if he was telling the truth, but I'm sure many will agree with me that he didn't have to sound his trumpet about it at his funeral. There may have been some who were impressed by his generosity but talking about it at the man's funeral was just in bad taste, as far as I'm concerned.

Besides the publicizing of their acts of generosity being morally distasteful to some of us, it puts the destitute beneficiary of their public generosity in the spotlight where everyone who looks on sees the appalling state that they may be in. The publicizing of the event exposes the recipients to the public glare and robs them of their dignity and self-respect. The mere prospect of such exposure might even discourage some from coming forward to claim the gifts that you may have for them. So the principle behind God's stance with regard to public doing of alms is a truly comprehensive and sound one.

There are further rules that God made on how we should dispense our money and wealth. This particular one rule has to do with how we treat our enemies. In Romans 12:20 we read the following: "*Therefore if thine enemy hunger, feed him: if he thirst, give him drink: for in so doing thou shalt heap coals of fire on his head {12:21} Be not overcome of evil, but overcome evil with good.* "

I know that some of that doesn't make a lot of sense and is somewhat unfathomable, but that is what is expected of you if you would walk with the Most High and be an heir to his estate. You are expected to show love and compassion not only to your family and friends because even the hypocrites and Pharisees do that. To be favoured by the Lord one must show kindness and mercy to one's enemies too. That is what impresses The One who gives us the means to feed the hungry and quench the thirst of the thirsty.

When the enemy who is dying of hunger and thirst rocks up at our door we must not chase them away but let them in and feed them. That way we overcome evil with good. This is one of those principles of which the taste is in the eating. Believe me it works, though it is not easy to internalize. It is one of the requirements for sharing in the vast heavenly inheritance, your responsibility as a child of God.

The next requirement we find in Matthew 6:5. Here it is: *"And when thou prayest, thou shall not be as the hypocrites are; for they love to pray standing in the synagogues and in the street corners, that they may be seen of men. Verily I say unto you, They have their reward. {6:6} But thou, when thou prayest, enter into thy closet, and when thou hast shut thy door, pray to thy Father which seeth in secret, and thy Father which seeth in secret shall reward thee openly.*

We are admonished against praying for the purpose of being seen and heard by people. When you enter into the house and close the door, you shut out the negative noises and enter into tranquillity of solitude. It says here that prayer should be a private matter between you and God. It goes without saying that the street corner prayers and those said to impress people in synagogues do not earn any reward from the Almighty. Only those said in private get rewarded.

Prayer shouldn't be said for the purpose of impressing anyone but directed straight to God, for His ears only. What is of note here is that thou you pray alone in a private place He rewards you in public, for all to see. In other words people will see that you are being rewarded but they will not know the reason for the reward.

God is here saying "let's keep the matter between the two of us. " I did say in a book in the series that He wants to work in a partnership with you. He wants you to have this special bond and understanding with Him so that He can win your battles for and with you. It is a relationship that does not involve any third party.

Let us move on to the next requirement. And we find it in Mark 11:25: "*And when ye stand praying, forgive, if ye have ought against any: that your Father which is in heaven may forgive you your trespasses {11:26} But if ye do not forgive, neither will your Father which is in heaven forgive your trespasses.*" This one is about prayer also. If this important requirement is not met then the prayer will not be acceptable to God, nor will it be answered as the one who says it wishes.

The reason behind this requirement is that we humans, all of us, are fallible creatures. None of us are perfect. We tend to make mistakes and in the process hurt each other. When we have done wrong we ask God for forgiveness, which He in His discretion and infinite wisdom will grant or deny us. This he does because He judges us with the same yardstick with which we judge others.

Therefore if we don't forgive those that trespass against us He will not forgive us. If we don't meet this requirement we will surely be saying prayers in vain when we say them and we would be thinking that He does not care about us anymore.

For your prayer for more wealth to be answered and for your desires to be fulfilled, make sure when you pray, that you do not have anyone you have not forgiven. That you are not holding any grudge against anyone. Only if you meet this all-important requirement will the rewards and blessings come your way.

In Proverbs 28:19 we read the following: "*He that tilleth his land shall have plenty of bread: but he that followeth after vain persons shall have poverty enough.* "Here is our safeguard against poverty, we have to work for what we want and not follow poor advice. We are guaranteed profits if we work on our projects. There has to be effort expended on our part for even the lottery winner did go and bet. There can be no reward for zero effort, with perhaps the exception of an inheritance from the estate of someone who is deceased. We who believe are urged to be workers and not expect something for nothing.

I come now to this somewhat strange requirement for a beneficial relationship with God, it is found in James 1:22 and reads as follows: "*But ye be doers of the word, and not hearers only, deceiving your own selves, {1:23} For if any be a hearer of the word, and not a doer, he is like unto a man beholding his natural face in a glass:{1:24} For he beholdeth himself, and goeth his way, and straightaway forgetteth what manner of man he was.*" I know, I also thought it a strange analogy, this of a man looking at himself in a mirror, who when he walks away from the mirror, immediately forgets what he looks like. It's comical.

Anyway we are here warned to hear the word of God and do as we are told and not listen only for entertainment, as it were. There are many who hear the word of God being preached, actively give consideration to its content, then walk away and do nothing about it. This makes them no better than those who have not heard the word at all. The word that is preached to a person who is a hearer of it only and not a doer thereof is like seed that is sown that falls upon a rock, doesn't take root and is eaten by the birds.

The value of the word is in its utility, if there is no doing of the word there can be no proving of its contents. In order to satisfy yourself as to whether or not the word is true you have to try it out for yourself. It cannot work for you if you do not use it.

You can never reap the benefits of the word if you do not do what it says, the same applies to reaping, to be able to reap, one must first sow. There can never be any fruit eating without first planting. For a person to grow in faith it is required that they be doers of the word.

In James 2:20-22 we read the following: *"But wilt thou know, O vain man, that faith without works is dead? {1:21} Was not Abraham our father justified by works, when he had offered Isaac his son upon the altar? {2:22} Seest thou how faith wrought with his works, and by works was faith made perfect?"* Without works there can never be any faith, for faith consists in doing as you believe. One can never have faith and do nothing about it. The value of faith is in the works, in doing things in accordance with one's belief.

If the word says that you must love your enemy and you on hearing it continue with your hatred for your enemy, you are not a doer of the word, but only a hearer of it. If the word says that you should love your neighbour as you love yourself and you do not love your neighbour after hearing this, you are only a hearer of the word and not a doer.

Faith grows by hearing and doing. This way you become a channel through which God's glory is manifested, if you are a doer of the word. Proverbs 10:21 reads as follows: *"The lips of the righteous feed many: but fools die for want of wisdom."* Listen and having heard, do as the word of God tells you to, so that you do not become one of those that standing knee deep in water, and are dying of thirst. Hear and do.

Chapter 5

Be aware: the Lord loves those who are kind to the poor

In Proverbs 14:31 we read the following: "*He that oppresseth the poor reproacheth his Maker, but he that honoureth Him hath mercy on the poor.*" {19:17} *He that hath pity on the poor lendeth unto the Lord; and that which he hath given will he pay him again.*" In as much as the Lord blesses and gives to those who ask to be given, He is always on the side of the poor and no one can expect much from Him who deals harshly with or does not have mercy for the poor.

When you oppress the poor, your conduct offends your Maker, you cannot honour your Maker when you don't have mercy on the poor. Oppression of the poor is a serious abomination to God. Kindness to the poor is the key to the door of God's heart. There is no way you can please Him if you have disregard and disdain for the poor. When you give to the poor, you receive your gift from God in return.

He loves the poor so much that He repays their gifts to those who give them. We are told that when you pity a poor person and give him/her some things, God will pay you for that which

you have given him/her. If it is money that you have given him/
her, God will pay you in cash.

We lose nothing by giving to the poor because whatever we give them is like a loan to God which He then repays us. This way He makes sure that we are not poorer for giving to the poor. He replaces what we give so that we do not have a shortage after giving to the poor. We suffer no loss by giving to the poor. This should encourage us to open our hearts and be givers when the situation calls upon us to be givers.

In Proverbs 21:13 we read the following: "*Whoso stopping his ears at the cries of the poor, he also shall cry himself, but shall not be heard.*" We are warned against ignoring the cries of the poor and we are told our turn to cry will surely come and if we have been oblivious to the cries of the poor, our cries will not be heard. That is what we are bringing upon ourselves when we don't heed the cries the poor.

Any way that you treat the poor, there are consequences. Reward or punishment as the case may be, carrot and stick. When you meet with a poor person or people, be careful how you treat them, because by your conduct towards them God will judge you.

Your attitude or conduct towards the poor could be the decider of whether or not God listens to and hears your prayers. And when prayers are not answered there is frustration, anxiety and unsatisfied wants and needs. You do not want to be on the receiving end of God's wrath for merely not having shown kindness to a poor person.

You don't want to forfeit your blessings by refusing to give a coin or two to a needy one. Perhaps that will henceforth be easier to do, now that we have a guarantee that we practically lose nothing by giving to the poor, that what you give to the poor is a loan to God, which He will duly repay. Imagine that pain and frustration of crying and not being heard.

In Proverbs 22:9 we read the following: *"He that hath a bountiful eye shall be blessed, for he giveth of his bread to the poor."* There are blessings galore for the charitable one who does not avoid eye contact with the poor because it is said of him that he gives of bread to the poor.

I don't want to sound like I'm telling people to bribe God with gifts to the poor because not every gift to the poor is deserving of a reward, only those gifts that are given with a cheerful heart are pleasing to God and He rewards only gifts given in this manner. So it's not like we can bribe him at all.

He looks into the heart of the giver. Gifts that are given dutifully and grudgingly do not count, so the giver in this case is in no better position than one who looked the other way or walked away without giving. There is no blessing for such a giver. If we do not have a bountiful eye, we can learn and train the eye that we have to be bountiful. There is no behaviour that cannot be learned, or unlearned, so take courage.

Proverbs 28:27 reads as follows: *"He who giveth to the poor shall not lack, but he that hideth his eyes shall have many a curse."* So there is no middle path, you either give to the poor and ensure that you lack nothing or look the other way and evoke many curses. So choosing the right thing to do by the poor is really a no brainer. There is no way to have a beneficial relationship with God if you are careless in your dealings with the poor. How you deal with the poor is a matter of critical importance. Your whole future depends on your attitude to poor people.

So we have to learn, if we are not yet, to be good consistent cheerful givers, everything depends on having a charitable heart. You cannot get away with refraining from giving to the poor, you don't want to face the dire consequences of your omission.

Chapter 6

The effect of various states of mind on us

In Proverbs 23:7 we read: "*⁶As he thinketh in his heart, so is he, Eat and drink, saith he to thee, but his heart is not with thee.*" Not even what we say with our mouths can belie what is in our hearts. As we think in our hearts, so we are. What we habitually think determines our mental attitude and our mental attitude determines our life conditions and circumstances. What we honestly think of ourselves, that we are.

Thoughts of abundance, wealth, good health produce in the thinker's life what they represent, they attract conditions and circumstances that are in harmony with them. I have heard it said that a person's attitude determines his/her altitude. I can't agree more with that sentiment. You cannot fly like an eagle if you think like a chicken. Your whole life is a reflection of what is constantly on your mind, it is a reflection of thoughts that are uppermost in your mind for the better part of your time.

We have before us at any given moment infinite options in terms of states of mind we can adopt and make our own. How we think about things determines our mental attitude. Our mental attitude determines whether we are winners or losers. It determines our station in life. It determines whether we are at the top or at the bottom. Oftentimes success starts with a change of mind and a decision to go after your goals.

But for a person who lives and walks by faith success starts with a prayer. When he prays he believes that he receives that which he is praying for or about and his state of mind changes from one of want to one of possession. As I have said previously, there is an intervening period between the saying of a prayer and the answering thereof.

In the intervening period the righteous sees him/herself in his/her mind as though he/she is already what he was desiring to be when he started to pray, as though he is already in possession of the thing he was praying for, in line with the principle outlined in Matthew 21:22. His conditions will change to be in harmony with his/her new state of mind.

In Philippians 4:6 we read the following: *"Be careful for nothing; but in everything by prayer and supplication with thanksgiving let your requests be made known unto God {4:7} And the peace of God, which passeth all understanding, shall keep your hearts and minds through Christ Jesus."* We are advised to be carefree in our attitude and not to be overly worried or overstressed about anything. That is the attitude made possible by the knowledge that with God nothing is impossible. When you put your trust in a Being to whom nothing is impossible, I don't see anything that could possibly stress or worry you for long.

We are to pray with thanksgiving, in other words we must have a mental attitude of gratitude even as we are making our requests known to God. Thanksgiving because we believe that our requests are already being responded to as we pray. We pray with the gratitude state of mind. And having prayed thus we are promised that the peace of God shall keep our hearts and minds through Christ Jesus.

We will have this peaceful state of mind from knowing that our requests have been addressed, we therefore are satisfied and no longer desire what we were praying for or about for the reason that you cannot continue to desire what you already have.

In the intervening period, in our minds we already are what we desired to be when we were praying, we are already in ownership of the thing we were praying for. Maintaining this state of mind throughout the entire intervening period is important for the realization of the desire in the physical world, in other words, for the manifestation or objectification of the object of our desire in the corporeal world.

Keeping the ownership thoughts uppermost in our mind for the better part of our time impresses the Subconscious mind with such thoughts so that it would then naturally act upon the impression and set in motion all the forces that are necessary for the objectification of the desired thing.

It is a natural process of interaction between the conscious and Subconscious mind that happens whether you are aware of it or not. Knowing the principles governing the relationship between the two minds we can act intentionally and deliberately to cause the conscious mind to make suggestions about the things that we want to the Subconscious mind that the latter will have no option but to act upon.

For this reason we have to be mindful of what diet we feed our minds. I can't stress that enough. In Matthew 6:34 we are given a bit of advice: *"Take therefore no thought for the morrow: for the morrow shall take thought for the things of itself. Sufficient unto the day is the evil thereof.*" To spend all your time today worrying and stressing about what you think is likely to happen tomorrow is often a futile exercise. Many of the things that we fear are about to happen in the immediate future do not happen at all or they don't happen as we expected them to when we were worrying.

Every day has trouble of its own that we should be dealing with on that particular day. Working today on solving the problems that arise today or have been carried over into today from yesterday ensures that tomorrow comes with fewer problems. But while you sit and worry about what might happen tomorrow, usually fearing the worst, today's problems remain unattended and you will be facing them again tomorrow, in addition to those that tomorrow will bring.

Living in fear of what might transpire tomorrow is not a wise way to live since we have no way of knowing exactly what tomorrow might bring. How many times have we stressed and worried, anxious about what we feared would surely happen in the near future because of what happened in the past or what may be happening presently, only to find that things don't go that way and perhaps the opposite of what we expected to happen, happens.

It is just as impossible to live in the future as it is to live in the past. We can only live in the present moment and we should therefore make the most of the time we have now and deal with tomorrow's problems when tomorrow comes.

In Matthew 6:27 we are asked a rhetoric question: "*Which of you by taking thought can add one cubit unto his stature?*" Here we are warned of the futility of worrying and stressing about things that we should be trusting God to help us with. The Bible tells us that God knows what we need before we even tell Him.

Jesus demonstrated this reality when he fed the multitude of people with a five loaves of bread and two fish. The Bible does not say that he prayed for God to increase the food, it says that he looked heavenwards, thanked God and broke the bread.

In addition to what I have stated above about the futility of worrying about what might transpire in the future, is the danger of unintentionally attracting to oneself the things feared. I have stated in a previous book just how powerful an emotion fear is. I will take this opportunity to reiterate that. A person who is afraid that something terrible is going to happen soon has very little capacity to focus his/her attention on anything else but the situation he/she is afraid of.

His/he mind is continuously fixated on the situation he/she fears would materialize. Thoughts of this dreadful future occurrence dominates his/her mind day and night, automatically making this impression on the Subconscious, which will make sure that the contents of the mental picture held in the conscious mind are manifested in the life of the thinker.

Thus that which the thinker focused his/her mind on will unfold in exactly the way he/she feared it would. So by excessively worrying about something bad that you fear might happen tomorrow, you might be unknowingly ensuring its eventual occurrence. You will never be able to add one cubit to your stature by taking thought.

This is very sound advice because the decisions that you take today and the actions that you take today directly influence what kind of day tomorrow will turn out to be. There is a definite connection between what happens today and what will happen tomorrow. If we work on making today alright we are automatically making tomorrow alright. If we do the land tilling and sowing correctly today instead of worrying whether it will rain or not tomorrow, we will be happy reapers in due season.

By our decisions and actions today we can determine what the future will look like. We can create the future that we want withour actions of today. If we get into the proactive state of mind and do all that we need to do today, tomorrow will have less troubles and when tomorrow becomes today and we do more of we did yesterday, or we carry on from where we left off, we are in effect creating the future we want. Don't worry about what tomorrow will bring, do what needs to be done now. The time you should be worrying about is now, worry about what you need to do now and do it now.

We can only live in the here and now. What happened yesterday is done and dusted, we will never live in that time again, it's gone past. Neither can we go into the future and do things there. We can only live in the eternally unfolding now. What you do now can make amends for what happened in the past and can certainly determine what the future will look like. Take no thought of the morrow, each day has enough trouble of its own.

Chapter 7
About dealing with loss

In closing, I want to talk about something that happens to all of us at some stage or another in our lives, and that thing is loss. At some point we all have to deal with loss of things that are precious and dear to us and it is therefore important that we learn to deal with loss in a way that shows that we know who and what we are in the scheme of things.

The topic brings to mind an occurrence that happened to me when I was in my early teens. My home was a brick house that did not have a ceiling, we had only a corrugated iron roof for the better part of my teenage years. Now, there were these tiny brown birds that used to build their nests at the top corners of our house and they were a source of great curiosity to me and my contemporaries as we were city dwellers and we had very limited variety of birds to see and know.

One day I came home from school to find one bird that had a nest at my home had somehow fallen into the house and couldn't find its way back to its nest. That was a very exciting sight that I saw that day and I immediately decided that I was going to chase and catch the bird and keep it as my pet. I immediately closed the door and started the chase, which ended in me eventually catching the bird.

I don't remember a time when I was more excited as a child. I had a bird that I was going to make my pet, and my bird and I were going to have a lot of fun together. I remember thinking how I would show off my pet to my friends. I was going to make them very envious. And then there was this woollen string that my aunt used to knit stuff with, I took it and cut a piece from it that was about a meter and a half in length. It was pink in colour.

I tied this string to the bird's leg and went outside to play with my pet. I released the bird while I held the tip of the string in my firm grasp. And the bird flew, unaware that it could only fly for the length of the string. I had myself a live kite, how cool can you get as a kid. I owned a brown bird which I flew like a kite.

I couldn't wait for my friends to see this amazing spectacle. But that was not to be, unfortunately for me and fortunately for the bird I guess, I unwittingly loosened my grip on the string, it slipped right out of my hands and my bird flew away and landed on a tree in the yard.

It had seated itself high up on the tree and I had no way of climbing to try and get hold of the string again because the tree branches where the bird sat were too thin, they wouldn't be able to support my weight. I stood there watching my bird on the tree, with the pink string still attached to its leg.

I was a very sad little boy who had lost his pet bird just minutes after finding it. After sitting there a few minutes the bird took off and flew away. I had lost my pet and I had to accept that it was gone. I was hurting badly. My ownership of the pet bird was very brief indeed and now I had lost it forever it seemed.

That was to be one of my earliest experiences of loss, but it taught me how to deal with loss at an early age. I knew from then that some things in life just slip through your fingers and fly away. To make matters worse for me, every day after I lost my bird I would see it fly by with the pink string still attached to it. It was still my bird but it didn't belong to me anymore.

Enough about that sad little boy story. There is this man in the Bible called Job. This man, once happened to be a subject of an argument between God and the devil we are told. Apparently God boasted to Satan about how faithful and loyal this man Job was to Him.

But the devil wasn't impressed and he told God that it was easy for Job to be faithful and loyal to Him because He had blessed him with children and great wealth. He apparently argued that if Job were to be stripped of everything that he had, his faith in and loyalty to God would end. He challenged God to strip Job of everything he had to see if he would continue to be faithful and loyal to Him. God apparently accepted the challenge.

Subsequently Job lost all his wealth and his children died. He became the poorest man in his community and God caused him to be covered with sores. We're told he was in such a terrible state that he shied away from people and kept pretty much to himself.

He had frequent visits from his friends though who tried to console, comfort and reassure him. That was quite a tall order as the man was hurting and wouldn't be consoled. Imagine having everything one day to wake up another day having absolutely nothing to your name.

That was Job's situation. But throughout the period of his extreme poverty, Job never lost his faith in God nor was he at any stage disloyal to Him. He protested and wailed much but his faith in God he kept resolutely. He cried and sobbed bitterly every day when he thought about all that he had lost.

And in the end his faith in God came through for him as God appeared to him and talked to him and his friends, we are told. God then restored his wealth. He blessed him with more than he had before. He gave him seven children and he blessed him with a long life. He lived to see his great grandchildren and died in ripe old age.

When we suffer loss, in whatever form, we should know that there must be a reason for that to happen to us and we must not begin to doubt God's love for us or His ability to restore what we may have lost. Loss of things that are dear to you invariably hurts and it is okay to go through the appropriate emotions but despair and helplessness must not overcome you.

We must remember that with God, nothing is impossible and that greater is He that is in us than the one that is in the world. This way we would have made our recovery form loss certain. We can dare to look forward to the restoration of what we may have lost. When we know the formula that we used to get what we have lost, recovery becomes a matter of again applying the formula. You can only be stressed about losing something if you don't know how you managed to be in possession of it. If you got it by sheer luck I guess that you cannot easily rinse and repeat.

www.ingramcontent.com/pod-product-compliance
Lightning Source LLC
Chambersburg PA
CBHW061404160726
47995CB00001B/451